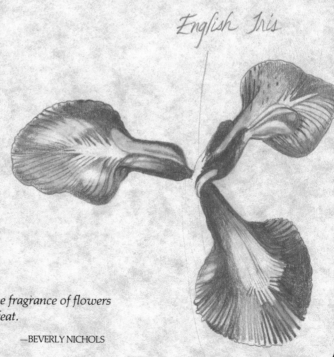
English Iris

To be overpowered by the fragrance of flowers
is a delectable form of defeat.

—BEVERLY NICHOLS

Trillium

Illustrated by Marie Garafano. Cover illustration by Pat Perleberg. Printed in the United States of America. Canadian representatives: General Publishing Co., Ltd., 30 Lesmill Road, Don Mills, Ontario M3B 2T6. International representatives: Worldwide Media Services, Inc., 115 East Twenty-third Street, New York, New York 10010. ISBN: 0-89471-331-0 (Paper). This book may be ordered by mail from the publisher). Please add $2.50 for postage and handling for each copy. But try your bookstore first! Running Press Book Publishers, 125 South Twenty-second Street, Philadelphia, Pennsylvania 19103.

FLOWER

Notebook

Kalanchoe

To analyze the charms of flowers is like dissecting music; it is one of the things which it is far better to enjoy, than to attempt fully to understand.

—HENRY THEODORE TUCKERMAN

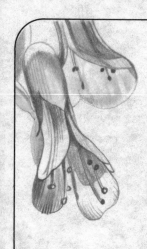

Flowers reflect the human search for meaning. Does not each of us, no matter how our life has gone, ache to have a life as beautiful and true to itself as that of a flower?

—PHILIP MOFFITT

The hellebores hibernate, full of promise, unexpected, precious, prostrate but fully alive. As long as the snow lies over them, they stay shut, ovoid, and on the outside of each bulgy petal, the vaguest suspicion of pink seems the only sign that they are breathing.

—COLETTE

Impatiens

The flowers of late winter and early spring occupy places in our hearts well out of proportion to their size.

—GERTRUDE S. WISTER

For in each of them one would be confronted by a miracle—the miracle that so tiny a thing should hold in its core a whole chalice of perfume, not yet distilled, and wings of white and gold that were floating about somewhere in infinity, or sleeping far below in the cool earth.

—BEVERLY NICHOLS

One of my grandfathers died of a clump of Iris stylosa; it enticed him from a sickbed on an angry evening in January, luring him through the snowdrifts with its blue and silver flames; he died of double pneumonia a few days later. It was probably worth it.

—BEVERLY NICHOLS

Foxglove

Flax

Flowers . . . are the poor man's poetry.

—ANNE PRATT

For three days I have been watching its largest bud, a tiny golden pod.
Tomorrow, the forsythia will be sprinkled all over with golden stars.

—KAREL ČAPEK

When worshippers offer flowers at the altar, they are returning to the gods things which they know, or (if they are not visionaries) obscurely feel, to be indigenous to heaven.

—ALDOUS HUXLEY

Begonia

A house with daffodils in it is a house lit up, whether or no the sun be shining outside. Daffodils in a green bowl—and let it snow if it will.

—A. A. MILNE

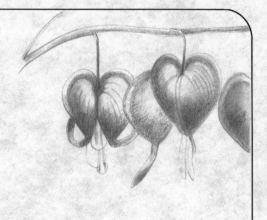

Bleeding Heart

Just as if an alarm set within the earth last fall had struck now, they must awake, they must arise, they must live. These plump daffodil buds, even if frozen solid tonight, will not bow in the morning.

—BERTHA DAMON

When I begin to write about flowers I lose all sense of restraint,
and it is far, far too late to do anything about it.

—BEVERLY NICHOLS

Are not flowers the stars of earth,
and are not our stars the flowers of heaven?

—ANONYMOUS

Tulip

Some of the richest colors of flowers . . . are produced by a crystalline or sugary frost-work upon them. In the Lychnis of the high Alps, the red and white have a kind of sugary bloom as rich as it is delicate. If you can fancy very powdery and crystalline snow mixed with the softest cream, and then dashed with carmine, it may give you some idea of the look of it.

—JOHN RUSKIN

*The ground is sodden sullen. The wind begins to howl. And suddenly—
violets, baskets of lacy violets amidst tiny furled leaves, green swords of
daffodil and tulip leaves, hyacinth knobs, forsythia in jets of gold, and red
handmade maple blossoms, rather thrown-together things, as though the
giant fingers of a tree cannot model a proper bright wax blossom.*

—DOROTHY EVSLIN

Canada Dogwood

*What a desolate place would be a world without flowers! It would be a face
without a smile, a feast without a welcome.*

—CLARA L. BALFOUR

A bud may be swollen to bursting, ready to open at any minute; but however long you stare at it, like the watched pot it won't boil until you turn your back.

—ELEANOR PERÉNYI

Fuchsia

The eyes of violets are full of dreams.

—COLETTE

Once we had a great pair of star magnolia bushes flanking the broad brick entrance walk to the front door. While these were in bloom we noticed that none but smiling faces greeted us, so great was the pleasure of mailman, delivery boy, and visitor in the unexpected fragrance that assailed them inside our gate.

—HELEN VAN PELT WILSON

Larkspur

In eastern lands they talk in flowers and tell
in a garland their loves and cares.

—JAMES GATES PERCIVAL

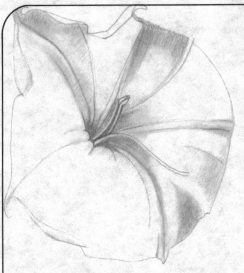

Jimson Weed

Flowers are restful to look at.
They have neither emotions nor conflicts.

—SIGMUND FREUD

If I had but two loaves of bread, I would sell one and buy hyacinths, for they would feed my soul.

—THE KORAN

I wish I could show you the hyacinths that embarrass us by their loveliness,
though to cower before a flower is perhaps unwise . . .

—EMILY DICKINSON

Cactus Flower
(Chain Fruit Cholla)

I desired the owner of the garden to let me know which were the finest of the flowers; for that I was so unskillful in the art, that I thought the most beautiful were the most valuable, and that those which had the gayest colours were the most beautiful.

—JOSEPH ADDISON

Wildflowers are perhaps the most enchanting of all for me. I love their delicacy, their disarming innocence, and their defiance of life itself.

—PRINCESS GRACE OF MONACO

The buttercup's face is burnished gold! No artist's paint nor printer's ink may copy that.

—F. SCHUYLER MATHEWS

Christmas Rose

I do not know of a flowering plant that tastes good and is poisonous. Nature is not out to get you.

—EUELL GIBBONS

Night - Blooming Cereus

Many summer standbys are already in flower before the end of May.
The last season of spring is also the first taste of summer's abundance.

—DENISE OTIS

Portulaca

Even the majestic cañon cliffs, seemingly absolutely flawless for thousands
of feet and necessarily doomed to eternal sterility, are cheered with happy
flowers on invisible niches and ledges wherever the slightest grip for a root
can be found; as if Nature, like an enthusiastic gardener, could not resist the
temptation to plant flowers everywhere.

—JOHN MUIR

Where a rose-pink peony will look "dirty" near a brilliant yellow iris, it is enhanced by juxtaposition to pink or blue lupines—the pink of the lupines has a tinge of blue in it, and the blue lupines have some red in their blue.

—BETTY POWELL and THOMAS POWELL

I would have taken care of daisies, giving them an aspirin every hour and cutting their stems properly, but with roses I'm reckless. When they arrive in their long white box, they're already in the death house.

—ANNE SEXTON

No flower is really understood until we have seen it both in the mass and individually; at a distance and in the hand.

—RICHARDSON WRIGHT

Magnolia

Roses are the only flowers that impress people at garden parties; the only flowers that everybody is certain of knowing.

—KATHARINE MANSFIELD

Water Lily

Summer to me always seems middle-aged compared with the adolescence of March, April, and even May.

—VITA SACKVILLE-WEST

The window was full of potted begonias, all pressing their pink noses against the glass.

—TAM MOSSMAN

Petunia

I like my geraniums to fight, to clash in eternal contests of colour, to wage their petalled arguments in perpetual debate, and in order that they do so there must be every sort of red, scarlet against magenta, cherry versus brick, crimson anti puce, etc.

—BEVERLY NICHOLS

Smell is the most memoristic of senses. The scent of a certain old-fashioned white rose inevitably recalls to me the great bush that grew by the back door of the house where I was born and how my little sister looked when she was just four years old.

—E. F. BENSON

Sweet-Scented Gladiolus

When it comes to beauty, I can think of nothing greater or more inspiring than a field of blooming marigolds tossing their heads in the sunshine and giving a glow to the entire landscape.

—SENATOR EVERETT McKINLEY DIRKSEN

Nearly everyone is interested to some extent in the flowers that grow around him; and, though many people are probably satisfied when they have learned to tell a rose from a buttercup, those who really love plants soon see more than the pretty posy and become aware of beautiful and significant structures within it.

—ANNE OPHELIA DOWDEN

Iris

The flower is the poetry of reproduction. It is an example of the eternal seductiveness of life.

—JEAN GIRAUDOUX

What a pity flowers can utter no sound! A singing rose, a whispering violet, a murmuring honeysuckle—oh, what a rare and exquisite miracle would these be!

—HENRY WARD BEECHER

Some flowers spoke with strong and powerful voices, which proclaimed in accents trumpet-tongued, "I am beautiful, and I rule." Others murmured in tones scarcely audible, but exquisitely soft and sweet, "I am little, and I am beloved."

—GEORGE SAND

Thunbergia

*The herbacious phloxes miraculously alter their hue as the evening light sinks
across them. I love color and rejoice in it, but white is lovely to me forever.*

—VITA SACKVILLE-WEST

Canterbury
Bells

*Now that the roses were in high bloom, the purple-blue
delphiniums stretched to peer over the tops of picket fences.*

—RODELLO HUNTER

Hast thou loved the wood-rose and left it on its stalk?

—RALPH WALDO EMERSON

Gloxinia

There are strange evenings when the flowers have a soul.

—ALBERT SAMAIN

There were those early breathtaking moments when the boy in your life sent a corsage before taking you to the school dance. It usually arrived in the morning and was kept fresh in its transparent container. I still have several of these corsages pressed flat with age. The corners of the roses are brown, and the maidenhair ferns fall to dust at the touch.

—PRINCESS GRACE OF MONACO

Phalaenopsis Orchid

When I meet a man who grows flowers, I have a tendency to believe that he will know who I am. Most men don't take the time and lack the imagination to notice who a woman really is, but a man who notices the color and the shapes of flowers is capable of noticing a woman.

—ANONYMOUS

When flowers are cut for the house, a carefully-nurtured border looks like hell for a while, and sometimes it never looks right again during the summer—to the fellow who plants it, I mean.

—AMOS PETTINGILL (WILLIAM B. HARRIS)

Try to keep a garden beautiful to yourself alone and see what happens—the neighbor, hurrying by to catch his train of mornings, will stop to snatch a glint of joy from the iris purpling by your doorstep. The motorist will throw on brakes and back downhill just to see those oriental poppies massed against the wall.

—RICHARDSON WRIGHT

Streptocarpus

Four-o'Clocks

*The flowers are nature's jewels, with whose wealth
she decks her summer beauty.*

—GEORGE CROLY

Daylilies colored orchid, cream, peach make me slightly sick, and the names are awful too: I would blush to admit I was growing Precious One, Disneyland, or Bitsy.

—ELEANOR PERÉNYI

Oxalis

When at last I took the time to look into the heart of a flower, it opened up a whole new world . . . as if a window had been opened to let in the sun.

—PRINCESS GRACE OF MONACO

This true old rose scent, the scent that has charmed humanity from time immemorial, is assuredly the most exquisite and refreshing of all floral odors— pure, transparent, incomparable—an odor into which we may, so to speak, burrow deeply without finding anything coarse or bitter, in which we may touch bottom without losing our sense of exquisite pleasure.

—LOUISE BEEBE WILDER

Flowers . . . have a mysterious and subtle influence upon the feelings, not unlike some strains of music. They relax the tenseness of the mind. They dissolve its rigor.

—HENRY WARD BEECHER

Every flower about a house certifies to the refinement of somebody. Every vine climbing and blossoming tells of love and joy.

—ROBERT G. INGERSOLL

Calla Lily

If we were to bring a tribute from our garden to one of whom we were fond, would it be a gargantuan African marigold and the biggest of the roses? No, it would be those flowers that are little and perfect.

—RICHARDSON WRIGHT

Whether you prefer masses of bloom or only a single flower depends on whether you are basically a painter or a sculptor.

—TAM MOSSMAN

Hollyhock

Flowers have an expression or countenance as much as men or animals. Some seem to smile; some have a sad expression; some are pensive and diffident; others again are plain, honest, and upright, like the broad-faced sunflower and the hollyhock.

—HENRY WARD BEECHER

Bellflower

Nobody sees a flower—really—it is so small—we haven't time—and to see takes time, like to have a friend takes time.

—GEORGIA O'KEEFFE

If I take a flower in my hand, I turn it round and round, wonderingly. I admire. I learn . . . But if I can draw it, I learn to love the ruffles on the edges of a petal, the curve of a filament, the lacework of the veining. I know the flower; it is now mine. Permanently and forever.

—MARTHA PRICE

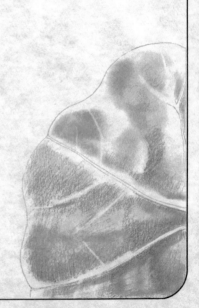

For a fantasy garden, the sunflower takes the prize. It's eerie. Somehow walking beneath a flower that towers some twelve feet above the ground—seven feet above my head, ten feet above my son's—invites games of imagination.

—SHARON MacLATCHIE

Nasturtium

It is so wrong to think of the beauty of flowers only when they are at their height of blooming; bud and half-developed flower, fading blossom and seed pod are lovely, and often more interesting.

—CLARE LEIGHTON

Chrysanthemum

Goldenrod has been unfairly condemned as allergy-inducing, an evil reputation it seems unable to shake off although it is entirely innocent.

—THALASSA CRUSO

The charm of asters is their fluffy heads and ravishing colors—dusty pinks and powder blues, strawberry reds and amethyst purples—and the way they arrange themselves in a bowl.

—ELEANOR PERÉNYI

Cyclamen

*One sure way to lose another woman's
friendship is to try to improve her flower arrangements.*

—MARCELENE COX

When you look at a flower, at a color, without naming it, without like or dislike, without any screen between you and the thing you see as a flower, without the word, without thought, then the flower has an extraordinary color and beauty.

—J. KRISHNAMURTI

I have noticed the almost selfish passion for their flowers that old gardeners have, and their reluctance to part with a leaf or a blossom from their family. They love the flowers for themselves.

—CHARLES DUDLEY WARNER

Marigold

Centaurea

*All flowers are lovely alone. And some flowers
are so beautiful in themselves that the addition
of another type distracts rather than adds interest.*

—J. GREGORY CONWAY

Late roses climbed and hung and clustered and the sunshine deepening the hue of the yellowing trees made one feel that one stood in an embowered temple of gold.

—FRANCES HODGSON BURNETT

One comes back to these old-fashioned roses as one does to music and old poetry. A garden needs old associations, old fragrances, as a home needs things that have been lived with.

—MARION PAGE

Mankind selects flowers for the expression of its finest sympathies, their beauty and fleetingness serving to make them the most fitting symbols of those delicate sentiments for which language seems almost too gross a medium.

—GEORGE STILLMAN HILLARD

Hybrid Tea Rose

"Why do my flowers look so sad today?" she asked, showing the student her bouquet of dying flowers.

He looked at it a moment before replying, "They have been dancing all night, and that is why they look so tired and hang their heads."

—HANS CHRISTIAN ANDERSEN

African Violet

In bloom anyone can see them, and even the crudest, hastiest visitor will note differences; but when they are not in flower, nobody comes to see and they are mine alone.

—L. H. BAILEY

Every autumn, when the new bulbs arrive, a proportion of them are handed out to any friends who may be around so that they may plant them in some secret place, where I can have the fun of discovering them in the spring. It is a sort of floral hide-and-seek which is very entertaining.

—BEVERLY NICHOLS

Pinks

As I write, snow is falling outside my Maine window, and indoors all around me half a hundred garden catalogues are in bloom.

—KATHARINE S. WHITE

Shasta Daisy

A flower without a name is a weed; a flower with a Latin name is somehow raised to a state of dignity.

—KAREL ČAPEK

Today, in all the turmoil of our world, we would do well to take some moments to dream of careless things—like spring and marigolds and the other flowers that soon will come.

—SENATOR EVERETT McKINLEY DIRKSEN

I look upon the whole country in spring-time as a spacious garden, and make as many visits to a spot of daisies, or a bank of violets, as a florist does to his borders or parterres. There is not a bush in blossom within a mile of me which I am not acquainted with, nor scarce a daffodil or cowslip that withers away in my neighborhood without my missing it.

—JOSEPH ADDISON

Orchid lovers turn cattleya purple if you suggest that they're anything but ornamental when out of bloom. And if you want to rile a begonia fancier, tell him that not every one is a beauty.

—VIRGINIA F. ELBERT and
GEORGE A. ELBERT

Scabiosa

The beauty of woodland wildflowers is that they exist at all. Finding a painted trillium or a pink lady's slipper elicits exclamations of admiration, as much from surprise that such a delicate flower is thriving unattended as from an appreciation of its form or color.

—ROGER B. SWAIN

Poppy

Anyone who will spend a few hours watching a blossom will discover things about its life-relationships that should amaze and delight him.

—ANNE OPHELIA DOWDEN

It takes years to exhaust the botanical treasures of any one considerable neighborhood, unless one makes a dead set at it, like an herbalist. One likes to have his floral acquaintances come to him easily and naturally, like his other friends. Some pleasant occasion should bring you together.

—JOHN BURROUGHS

English Daisy

Stars will blossom in the darkness,
Violets bloom beneath the snow.

—JULIA DORR

Columbine

*Hyacinth and dwarf iris and narcissus—bulbs I planted two Thanksgivings
ago through snow six inches deep, and now look at them!*

—BERTHA DAMON

Men plant flowers because it represents a way of affirming the renewability of life—watching them grow each year, you know you can do it again next year.

—ANONYMOUS

The flowers rose like priests, solemnly bowing their heads, defying frost and wind. "There is no death," they were declaring. "There is no death!"

—CONSTANCE ARMFIELD

And the roses—the roses! Rising out of the grass, tangled round the sun-dial, wreathing the tree trunks and hanging from their branches, climbing up the walls and spreading over them with long garlands falling in cascades . . . they came alive day by day, hour by hour.

—FRANCES HODGSON BURNETT

Dahlia

Narcissus

Where would we be if humanity had never known flowers? If they didn't exist or had always been hidden from our sight . . . would our character, our morals, our aptitude for beauty, our happiness be the same?

—MAURICE MAETERLINCK

Like snow, dandelions enchant children but dismay adults.

—BARBARA POND

Sweet Peas

Arranging a bowl of flowers in the morning can give a sense of quiet in a crowded day—like writing a poem, or saying a prayer.

—ANNE MORROW LINDBERGH

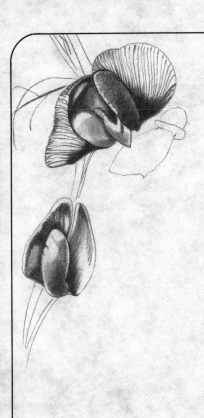

*Look! Aren't they cute? And to think
I found them in a vacant lot!*

—LESTER ROUNDTREE

So much of the beauty of a flower is in its very perishableness.
One doesn't want it to last forever and accumulate dust.

—DENISE LEVERTOV

Evening
Primrose